# Contents

Appendix

- Example of value time table
- Uses of meditation

# Introduction

Time is the most valuable gift that god gave us. Nothing can exist without time and we all know that time never stops, it always moves forward and what happens in past we can't change it.

Using time for achieving goals is a good thing but many people failed to do this because time is like a moving rocket you can use that rocket to go to moon, mars, Saturn etc but this can only happen when you know how to drive the rocket to your desired direction, and which fuel is need for rocket and if there is a problem in the rocket then you need to know to solve that problem so, there are many things you need to learn to go to moon, mars, Saturn etc similarly, if you want to achieve your goal then you need know how to use time, in other words, how to manage the time and what is the value of time. So, before understanding what is the value of time? How to manage time? Let us know what is time?

## What is time?

Time doesn't have any fixed definition even in physics, because time is beyond what we think but we have given it a measuring unit called seconds 60 seconds make a minute and 60 minutes make an hour and 24 hours make 1 day. We say this because earth takes 23 hours 56 minutes and 4 seconds to do one rotation but do you think is there enough time to achieve anything? If you say no then how did your role model achieve this many things?

You didn't achieve in your life because you neither know the value of time nor its management so, let us learn both of them in this book. But why is knowing value and management important?

## Importance of time value

Let's assume you have two cars. One is of 200000$ and the other is 3000000$, in this I ask one car should be destroyed then what will be your choice? Most or everyone will give the 200000$ car to be destroyed because we know that the value of it is low. Similarly, when we know the value of time we won't let it destroy our time, in other words we won't waste our time. These fears of getting time destroy keeps us motivated to work hard.

Even knowing the value of time makes you to carefully manage the time because when you know that (from the previous example) you are using a 3000000$ car then you will definitely manage that carefully.

**Importance of time management**

Let us take this by the same example of car you have, the car of worth 3000000$ and you know its value, you have maintained it in a very good way, the fuel is full, the car's battery is full, the interior is clean, the engine is performing good and you sit inside the car, inserts the key, starts the car and the car sounds vroom, vrooom and then you realise that *"you don't know to drive the car"*

Here, many people won't understand that is management driving a car or maintaining the car. In the terms of car it's maintaining but in the terms of time it's driving to your desired direction or using for you desired task effectively.

Even management of time helps in taking sudden decision even when there is an emergency, because when you know what you should do in your upcoming time suddenly you encounter a problem and you can immediately change your routine because you have learnt how to manage the time.

So, this is the introduction to the value and management of time now let us know what is the value of time?

# Value of time

Value, everything in the world as its own value some value can be measured and some value can't be measured.

If you what to know the value of time you need to

follow a strict time table in which the tasks need to be your loved ones or the tasks which you are interested, just for a week, like learning new language, learning new skills, once I did this experiment and I destroyed my 70 percent laziness.

Just follow this strict routine for a week, this routine helps you to understand the value of time because in this strict routine you will start feeling that the time is very less and you will get to know the immeasurable value of time. And there is one more way where you can get to know the immeasurable value of time in 10 minutes; you need to off your TV, no noises, no songs, no audio. Next sit any where you feel comfortable and set a timer of 10 minutes then close your eyes don't open your eyes until the timer rings, don't sleep, don't do any activity, after 10 minutes open your eyes and you will get to know the how long is 10 minutes.

From this 10 minute experiment or the strict time table experiment you got to know the immeasurable value of time but how to get to know the measurable value of time. Let us learn this in the next topic.

# Units of value of time

The measurable value of time, let us understand with our pervious example of rocket, there we know that we need to put the fuel to the rocket to move so, this means the value which you can measure is what you give at certain period of time, let us understand with another example.

Once you went to buy 1kg of rice, at one shop which is next to your house the price is 12$ and in another shop which is 1 kilo meter away from your house the price is

10$ per kg so, you go to the cheap priced shop and buy 1 kg of rice in a queue because it's cheap many people would come there and you come back after 40 minutes now the value you gave for 40 minutes is just 2$.

After reading this example many people think that we should save time and buy everything near as possible, but it's wrong thought because in the same case when you go to buy 100 kg of rice, then if you buy in the shop which is 1 kilo meter far from your home then you would spend 100 multiplied by 10 is equal to 1000$ but when compared to near shop the difference is 200$ so, for the same 40 minutes you gave 200$ value!

So, the value varies every time when your action

varies, this is way people say that "think before you act"

 We have understood the measurable value of time varies but are money only the measurable value of time?

No, there are 2 more measurable value of time, let us know them with an example.

You ate a lunch of worth 2$ in 15 minutes so, the value

you gave for this 15 minutes is negative 2$ which means you lost 2$ so, eating lunch would cause lose then will you leave eating lunch? Definitely not because you lost money but you gained energy of 500 calories so, the value of 15 minutes is gain of 500 calories and loss of 2$ so, the another unit to measures the value of time is energy.

Now, last one measuring unit is left, let us know this also by an example.

Every day you work a lot and your value of time, in terms of money increases and energy decreases after that you sleep but while sleeping you will earn money? Or will you earn energy? No, you won't gain anything because they both stay at zero. Then why to sleep?

Why many people say that sleeping is important?

Whenever you do a task you gain stress even if it is your most interested task. Your one whole day has work and has a lot of stress. So, to release that stress we need to sleep, so, the third unit of measurable value of time is stress, in a day you gain stress a lot, gain money a lot and loss energy a lot. At night while sleeping you lose stress, no money gain and no energy gain. But what is the use of this let us know more about it in next chapter.

# Value time table

You all might have come across the time table but what is the value time table here you represent the value of time in the form of numbers, before knowing how to use value time table? Let us know what is the use of value time table?

## What is the use of value time table?

In a company the chief executive officer (CEO) always can't keep an eye on his employees especially in companies where employees are more than 1000 so, CEO checks the statistics of the company to track their employees

For us also we can't keep an eye on time every time so, keeping a track on the value which you give for time, helps you to get to know about yourself and your work.

 Now let us know how to make the value time table?

## How to make the value time table?

To make the value time table you need to follow the following steps:

- Take a sheet of paper, in that you need to make 4 columns.

- In the four columns the first column shows the time, each 30 minutes, for example I get up at 5 am so my first column will be 5 am to 5:30 am,5:30 to 6 am, 6am to 6:30

am.......8:30pm to 9 pm, here I have chosen 9pm because I sleep at 9 pm.

- The 2nd row represents money, 3rd row represents energy and 4th row represents stress.

- Before you sleep you can just recall your day and write how much value you gave for every 30minutes for each rows ( stress can be rated in the scale of 0 to 100)

- If you still did not understood you can see the appendix 1 where an example of value time table is give.
  Now, we know how to make the value time table but the question is how to use this for our self growth?

## How to use the value time table?

Firstly, you need to have at least 7 days of value time table because if you have more data then you can have a clearance to take decision, next you need to check, on an average how much value you give in terms money, energy and stress per day. This helps you to understand yourself better and better and even you can make your 7 day value time table every 6 months ones so, that you can track you growth and your performance using this value time table. Now, we know about the value time table now let us know the 2 paradoxes of time.

# Time paradoxes

Time never goes as we want. Time has its own speed; it never stops and never gets reversed, but subconsciously some changes takes place in time.

Here, let us call these laws as paradox because they are only valid subconsciously not in reality but don't think that if it's not valid in reality then it's no use.

Let us learn our first paradox using an example

Assume you are driving a car. In a car we have an input component called accelerator, you may have observed that when you press your accelerator and stop at some point and you won't change your foot position, here the acceleration is constant but even if acceleration is constant the speed will be increasing as time goes.

Here we saw that higher the acceleration higher the speed this happens even in our real life, have you ever noticed that while you're doing your interested task or an important task time moves faster and faster but in reality the time didn't become fast and I call this paradox as **the acceleration paradox.** Let us know why this happens.

**The acceleration paradox**

In this paradox time won't become fast you become very slow in your work because of extreme focus. When you have a good focus then you subconscious time becomes slow and you won't even do a minor multitasking so, your inner functioning slows down but your uncontrolled superpower the subconscious mind becomes active in the work so, your productivity will increases and you give your best at this time but when you see the time, the time will be more than you think. Now we know 1 paradox let us know the other one.

Let us the 2$^{nd}$ paradox with an example. Let us take the same example of car. When your speed increases rapidly, the engine of the car heats up rapidly, because every car has a max speed if you try to accelerate more then there is a very high chance of engine failure after engine failure and we can't move our car so, the car makers have made a cooler in cars engine, this decreases the chances of engine failure and can able to accelerate for long time.

Here the engine is your brain, the speed is your subconscious time and the engine failure is the headache or de-energetic but we don't know what the cooler is? Let us know it.

But we also know that our brain uses 20% oxygen of our body to function in a proper manner so, our 2$^{nd}$ paradox is the cooler paradox.

## The cooler paradox

Have you observed that when you breathing slowly makes your subconscious time move slowly? This happens because our brain starts doing task in cool and calm way because our brain gets the sufficient oxygen so, you need to breathe 15 to 20 breathe per minute so, that your brain need to be cool and healthy. If your brain is cool and healthy the subconscious time slows down so, at this situation your mind will be open and for you time moves slow, at this time if you accelerate which means focus you can focus for a long time and productivity increases . Now, we know the two paradox of time but how to use them let us know it now.

## How to use the two paradoxes?

To use the two paradoxes you need to combine them here we can notice one thing that the two paradoxes are done subconsciously so, the combination is also done subconsciously.

Most of the people breathe 25 to 30 breathe per minute for them they can't use both the paradoxes at a time because both of them need focus and you can't focus both at a time. So, you need to make anyone paradox as your habit. You can't make the first paradox as your habit but you can make the second paradox as a habit which means that you need to do this habit commonly or else you need do the habit subconsciously, let us know more about it.

Here, the above paragraph says that you need to make your slow breathing as a habit, breathing is common, everybody does it but instead of 25 to 30 breathe per minute let us do 15 to

20 breathe per minute. Here the question is how?

When we talk about breathing and focus we get one of the main task comes in our mind. Your guess may be wrong or right but I think you guessed it correctly I am saying about meditation. Many of them have tried to do meditation and left to do mediation because they wanted result of meditation very fast or they stared to do long duration at the beginning days of meditation. Now let us know the correct way to do mediation.

To do meditation you need to follow three simple steps

- First, gain the calmness, you just need to take a deep breath just twice this makes our brain able concentrate
- Next , whenever you have a free time just sit

straight ( sit on floor not on chair and have a mat underneath ) and close your eyes

- Next, take a deep breath, the air need to fill your lungs, then release it and do this action for 3 minutes, just 3 minutes.

**Note:** never open your eyes while doing meditation.

Many may think that we won't get much result. Yes, you are right; we won't get much result until unless we do a 15 to 30 minute meditation but don't think that these three steps are useless because I think that if you want to go to moon then first we need to reach clouds, so we need to put the 30 sec instalment. Now what is 30 sec instalment let us know more about it.

When you start doing meditation for 3 minutes after 2 to 3 days add 30 sec more then you should meditate 3:30 minute and after 2 to 3 days you need to add another 30 sec which means 4:00 like this you need to do until it reaches 15 to 30 minutes.

By this way you will get the habit of slow breathing and meditation.

Meditation has many others uses too which is in the appendix 2. Now you can use both paradoxes at a time and get more productive and value your time correctly.

Now let us move towards management

# Time management

Management of time is one of the most important skills in the universe. If you know to manage you time then you can achieve your goal in a quick and better manner.

Management of time helps you to use your 86,400 seconds effectively and makes your mind stress free when you take your next step because you would already know your next step and it will be clear. Now let us know the next concept of time management.

# The concept of smart work

Smart work, everyone talks about this topic that don't do hard work do smart work but do you know what is the difference between hard work and smart work? Do you think we should not do hard work?

If I want to say the answer in six words then my answer is "hard work is the only way to success", then what is smart work?

Smart work means the hard work done using time management. Let us know more about it.

Have you ever observed that you can do some work effectively at some period of time but not in every time and when you get to know about your productive time where you can do your work effectively and you work on that time, that's what is called smart work .now let us know how to find you best time to work?

Everyone has their own productive time where they can do their work effectively but everybody in the world has a common time where they are effective and that time is 'morning'. Let us know more about it.

## Why is morning more productive time?

Morning is more productive time because you will be at zero stress stage. If you have read the value time table then you know that when we sleep we release our all stress so, at morning we will have a zero stress brain and we can do our work effectively.

Now many of them would have a question that is there any technique from which we can do effective work even in afternoon and evening, the answer is "I have a technique for it"

We know that after sleeping when we wake up we are in a zero stress stage so, this makes us productive at the morning, can we say that if we sleep afternoon once then we will be productive all time?

Never, you won't gain productivity after sleeping in afternoon but you may gain some laziness, then what should we do?

There is a technique which can get an energy of 2 hour sleep within 2 minutes but before that let us know when should we try this technique?

You should not do this technique just after food, here just means 1 to 2 hours.

You should not try this technique before exercise but you should try this technique after exercise. Now, let us know the technique.

Firstly, lay down in the supine position. Next, keep the foot 1 to 2 feet apart with the toes pointed outwards. Next, place the hands about 6 inches away from the body; keep the head in a straight and comfortable position. Next, gently close the eyes and start breathing slowly. Next focus on your legs and try to release the stress in legs, after legs focus on your arms then release the stress in your arms and same with the torso and head.

Do this technique for 2 minutes and you will get energy of 2 hours and this is a yogasana know as shavasana. Shavasana means relax posture where the body looks like shava or corpse. Now let us go to the next topic.

# The switch time rule

Focus is one of the important things to achieve success. But changing the direction of focus from one task to another is very much difficulty because if our brain addicts with one task then it takes a lot of energy to change your focus. so, let us know a trick that can change your focus from one task to another which is less energy consuming and use full too.

Let us know this trick with an example, let us use the car example, in manual cars there is a gear rod which helps you to change the gear, but before that you need to press the clutch to change the gear. Now, the question is why we need to press clutch to change the gear?

Because by pressing the clutch the connection between the engine and the gear box cuts off and after changing gear you will leave the clutch so, that the connection should be back.

So, here we got to know that our brain is engine, our task is the gear and what is the clutch?

The clutch is what I call the switch time. Switch time means the time where you switch from one task to another. Before understanding switch time let us know what is multitasking and switch tasking

Multitasking (in terms of the previous example), when you drive a car using two gears at a time is called multitasking. In reality we can't put two or more gears at a time but we can do 2 or more task at a time like eating food and watching TV at a time and this is multitasking, this will not leave you to enjoy neither food nor TV and please don't do multitasking.

But we can do switch tasking. Switch tasking means switching from one task to another like first eating food and next watch

TV and not doing both the task at a time. Now, let us know the switch time.

Switch time is a period of time in which you switch from one task to another like if you want your mind to change a task, from eating food to watching TV that period of time where you switch from eating food to watching TV is switch time, eating to watching tasks fraction of seconds to switch task but what if we need to switch subjects like from maths to history it's very difficult because high energy is taken by brain so, what should we do?

Here also you need to use the switch time for example you want to read maths and history then you think of starting to study maths on 3 pm and after an hour ( 4 pm) you will go start history here there is no sufficient switch time so, we need to add sufficient switch time for example, 3 pm I will start studying maths and from 3:55 pm to 4:05 pm is switch time and 4:05 pm to 5 pm I will study history so, from this example we get to know that the switch time for subject is 10 minutes so, I split the 4 pm switch time to 3:55 pm to 4:05 pm but the question is, does every task have same switch time? What should we do in that switch time? Let us know about it.

## Does every task have same switch time?

No, every task switch time won't be the same for example; to switch from eating food to watching TV it doesn't even take a second but in case of maths and history it takes 10 minutes so, how to know the switch time of every task?

**The higher the brain usage the higher the switch time**

if a tasks uses much brain means to switch that task you need more time for example, in our first case which is eating food to watching TV there while eating food you brain is used for very less energy consumed task like sensing the taste etc so, more switch time is not required but in the case of maths to history you use your brain lot like creativity, memory etc so, switching task is difficult and we need a 10 minutes of switch time. Now let us know what should we do in this switch time?

## What should we do in that switch time?

Let us know its do's and don'ts while switch time.

## Do's

* Stay away from the previous task for example (maths and history case), you should not read maths or stay away from maths.
* Drink a glass of water.
* Do walking.

* Do stretch exercises.

**don'ts**

* Don't sit.

* Don't use screen like mobile, TV etc.

And after 70 percent switch time you can start your next task for example (maths and history case), after 7 minutes (70 percent of time) of switch time you can start glancing history so that brain starts recalling the memory of history and you can switch you task easily. Let us move to our next concept.

# Time table rules

Time table is important to achieve any goal so, time table is necessary for everyone. But do you know the better way to make time table that helps you in any situation. Let us know the rules to make time table.

**1. Apply the switch rule**

You know what switch time is so; you can use it in your time table.

## 2.  The plan B

You always need to have a plan B, many people say we should not have plan B because they confuse between plan B and goal B, which means that if something goes wrong then change the way not the goal, here the 2nd way is our plan B. your plan B should be simple and not much risky because plan B is only meant to come back to your normal stage and try plan A again.

## 3.  Non periodic rule

So, you all know the periodic rule that if one task is done today then the same task should be done tomorrow at the same time, but this can't be applied for whole day, you should only apply it for daily routines like wake up, breakfast etc let us know why in our chapter.

# The limit rule

Let us know my own story to know this rule.

When I was studying in my higher primary classes I didn't like to study so, I would get less marks and I also watched a lot of TV so, my mother said me "from today you will study 1 hour from 7 pm to 8 pm and in other time you may watch TV" but my father said "don't set time limits for studying set time limits for TV in all other time he should study" but I used this in a different way and which can be used by everyone and that rule is **set limits for other things not for work and learning** , set limits to sleep, social media etc not for work and learning so, for what all you have set limits for that you can apply periodic rule. Now let us move towards appendixes.

# Appendix 1

# Example of value time table

A man sleeps 9.5 hours a day from 9pm to 6:30 am. The value time table will be

| time | money($) | energy(cal) | stress(0 to 100) | task |
|---|---|---|---|---|
| 6:30 am to 7 am | -30 | 0 | 0 | wake up, bath |
| 7 am to 7:30 am | 0 | -200 | 30 | exercise |
| 7:30 am to 8 am | -20 | 500 | 10 | breakfast |
| 8 am to 8:30 am | -30 | 0 | 45 | news |
| 8:30 am to 9 am | -50 | -15 | 40 | getting ready |
| 9 am to 9:30 am | 10 | -15 | 20 | job |
| 9:30 am to 10 am | 10 | -15 | 22 | job |
| 10 am to 10:30 am | 10 | -15 | 24 | job |
| 10:30 am to 11 am | 10 | -15 | 26 | job |
| 11 am to 11:30 am | 10 | -15 | 28 | job |
| 11:30 am to 12 am | 10 | -15 | 30 | job |
| 12 pm to 12:30 pm | 10 | -15 | 32 | job |
| 12:30 pm to 1 pm | -25 | 500 | -50 | lunch |
| 1 pm to 1:30 pm | 10 | -15 | 10 | job |
| 1:30 pm to 2 pm | 10 | -15 | 10 | job |
| 2 pm to 2;30 pm | 10 | -15 | 10 | job |
| 2:30 pm to 3 pm | 10 | -15 | 10 | job |

| 12 pm to 12:30 pm | 10 | -15 | 32 job |
| 12:30 pm to 1 pm | -25 | 500 | -50 lunch |
| 1 pm to 1:30 pm | 10 | -15 | 10 job |
| 1:30 pm to 2 pm | 10 | -15 | 10 job |
| 2 pm to 2;30 pm | 10 | -15 | 10 job |
| 2:30 pm to 3 pm | 10 | -15 | 10 job |
| 3 pm to 3:30 pm | 10 | -15 | 10 job |
| 3;30 pm t0 4 pm | 10 | -15 | 10 job |
| 4 pm to 4:30 pm | 10 | -15 | 10 job |
| 4:30pm to 5 pm | 10 | -15 | 10 job |
| 5 pm to 5:30 pm | -2 | 5 | -30 snack breac |
| 5:30 pm to 6 pm | 10 | -15 | 10 job |
| 6 pm to 6:30 pm | 10 | -15 | 10 job |
| 6:30 pm to 7 pm | 10 | -15 | 10 job |
| 7 pm to 7:30 -pm | -10 | 0 | 20 back to hom |
| 7:30 pm  to 8 pm | -10 | 0 | 5 tv |
| 8 pm to 8:30 pm | -30 | 600 | 2 dinner |
| 8:30 pm to 9 pm | -10 | 0 | 5 tv |

And from 9 pm to 6:30 am
he loses his all stress.

This is just an example but you can make your own value timetable according to your time table.

# Appendix 2
## Uses of meditation

- Elimination of tension, pressures and stress of a day to day life.
-  You get Control on your anger, pain, sadness and irritability.
- Increases consistency, confidence, concentration, memory, positive thinking.
- Better social behaviour.

- Flushes the cancer causing radiation from brain and body, radiated by cell phones, computers etc.
- Prevention of Alzheimer.

So, you learnt to manage the time but do you know to gain success then there is book of mine called

**"Theory of success: laws of success"**

An there is another book of mine in which I have mentioned how to get rid of Laziness and that book is

**"Kill your greatest enemy laziness: a 15 day war between you and laziness"**

........thank you for reading..........

www.ingramcontent.com/pod-product-compliance
Lightning Source LLC
Chambersburg PA
CBHW061703130726
47996CB00006B/2132